MENC The National Ass[...]
MUS[...] EDUCA[...]

It Works for Me!

The National Anthem and Other Patriotic Music in the Classroom

A special thanks to DaimlerChrysler and
the Jeep® brand for their generous support of
the National Anthem Project.

Production Editor: Teresa K. Preston

MENC: The National Association for Music Education
1806 Robert Fulton Drive
Reston, VA 20191

Printed in the United States of America
ISBN 1-56545-168-6

CONTENTS

Preface

Music has the power to unite a nation as citizens join their voices in harmony, expressing their affection and respect for the nation they all share. In order to join together in song, citizens must learn the songs of their common heritage. Unfortunately, many Americans remain silent simply because they do not know the songs we all share. A 2004 Harris interactive poll found that almost two-thirds of Americans do not know the U.S. national anthem. Some do not even realize that the song has more than one verse.

American music teachers share the task of helping young Americans learn these songs. And many have been incredibly successful. In fact, the Harris poll found that 70 percent of Americans who know the U.S. national anthem learned it in their school music classes. MENC: The National Association for Music Education hopes to spread that success through its National Anthem Project, a campaign being launched in 2005 to help Americans learn—or relearn—"The Star-Spangled Banner." (Go to www.nationalanthemproject.org for more information on the National Anthem Project. The site includes a bulletin board where you can share your own ideas for teaching the national anthem.)

In this book, music teachers who have been successfully teaching the national anthem and other songs of our national heritage share their secrets for success. These teachers have shared what works for them in hopes that these ideas will work for teachers across the nation. Together, the music teachers of the nation can help all citizens lift their voices (and instruments!) in celebration and pride.

As you peruse the ideas in this book, you will no doubt notice that teachers have diverse, and sometimes even conflicting, ideas on how to best approach this music. For example, some teachers abhor the modern pop arrangements of "The Star-Spangled Banner" often heard before ball games; others use recordings of such performances to encourage students to take an interest in learning the song. Use the ideas that will work best for you and your students. MENC members can join the dialogue about patriotic music in the classroom by participating in the member communities at www.menc.org. There you can share your opinions, ask questions of other music teachers, and learn more about what music teachers throughout the U.S. are doing in their classrooms.

We at MENC hope you find a lot of great ideas in this volume and that you will be on the lookout for future compilations of teacher ideas and success stories on a variety of topics in upcoming installments of the "It Works for Me!" series.

MAKING PATRIOTIC MUSIC

Respect and National Pride

"The Star-Spangled Banner," "America the Beautiful," and other patriotic songs are familiar to many American schoolchildren before they learn them in music class. They've heard the national anthem at ball games, sometimes performed by pop singers or in front of an unruly crowd eager for the game to start. Some students—and teachers—may think the national anthem is too difficult to sing or that the patriotic standards are no longer worthy of respectful attention. Teachers often have to take the time to teach proper etiquette and generate interest and excitement about patriotic music. But many of those teachers have found that their efforts have paid off.

■ Many of my students come to love the USA's patriotic songs because of my passion for the songs. For some students, my introducing them to these songs is their first introduction to any patriotic music of the USA, and I feel it's important for me as a musician and music teacher to share these songs with them.

■ Our first discussion, before truly delving into the national anthem, is about pride. Do students understand the term and can they put it in their own words? How do we show our pride for something? How do we show our pride as Americans?

■ Students have questioned why they have to learn the national anthem. I find that many students either have forgotten the verses, don't know there are multiple verses, or only know that it's related to sports. Before presenting the music to the students, I give anticipatory questions with a short reading of how the anthem came about and a short history lesson that includes information on the writer. An open forum classroom discussion follows their question of why they have to learn it. Then higher-order thinking processes begin, and students basically answer their own question.

■ We talk about what the anthem is used for and why it's important to have one. My students continue to surprise me with well-thought-out answers about the purpose of the anthem and why it would be weird not to have one.

■ I have always thought it was important for children to know and respect their national anthem. We discuss particularly the Olympic games, the use of national anthems there, and the fact that most countries have a national anthem. I also play a little of several (Canada, France, Britain) for them to hear.

■ When talking about the national anthem, I always do a short lesson on national anthems of other countries. (We are a very international school.) Using my *National Anthems of the World* book, I'll ask students to tell me what country their family is from, then we play and sing part of the anthem. (Some of them know it!) This reinforces the fact that every country has an anthem, and that it has meaning for that particular country.

■ We talk about the fact that some people think that another song should be chosen for the national anthem. "The Star-Spangled Banner" is too long, too hard, too high, too hard to memorize, etc. We then have a debate and vote on our preference. "The Star-Spangled Banner" always wins.

■ There are rules they need to understand and follow for the national anthem, which is a concept some students are not familiar with. Hats need to come off. They need to stand to sing this song, even if they are still learning it. They need to face a flag in the room even if there is one pictured in their book. It is also out of respect that they say the correct words, which means their books are held high enough to still see the flag.

■ I ask my students to always be the example setters when singing the anthem for the rest of their lives. I encourage everyone always to sing the national anthem as "their most respectful selves, using their most respectful voices," to focus on the flag and help *others* stay focused: keep as still as possible, keep your eyes on the flag (or written words) and think about what you're singing. I also discuss how to handle someone wanting to talk to them or "act silly" during the singing of the anthem at a baseball game or anywhere (like the classroom). I tell them: "Just keep your eyes on the flag, keep singing, shake your head slightly and hold up a finger to mean 'Hold on, please wait until the end of the song.'" Placing them all in the role of example setters before we sing has great preventive effect. I usually add: "I'm all for being silly when it's time to be silly—but during the national anthem, well, it's just not the time … it's the time to focus on the country we live in, and the flag, and how lucky we are that it's still waving in front of us. Yes?" When I see the nods and grins, I know it's time to sing.

■ I stress the etiquette—no hats, respectful singing, face the flag, "play ball" is not part of the lyrics, etc.

■ I've told the boys in my class that it would be a disgrace to be on a football team and stand at attention and have the television camera zero in on their mouth only to find they don't know the words! After this, the boys began to stand in "football team" position as they sang and envisioned themselves as the very best athlete on the field of play.

■ I stress the importance of singing it with dignity and pride—not to treat it like a pop song or to sing it with their own vocal inflections. Many young singers have probably only heard pop singers perform this piece, so they think that's the only way it should be sung. They have no idea of what it could sound like if sung by a trained singer.

■ I am opposed to the recent embellishments the performers of today have added to the song. I feel that it is *our* national anthem and should not be a performance piece. I would rather see every athlete singing, rather than standing silently in a reverent position. I would like to see the Olympic winners singing along with the entire audience. In addition to including the singing of the national anthem at the beginning of the school day, perhaps we should encourage unison singing at little league games through college functions and encourage people to realize the song is an anthem for all to sing.

■ I discuss with the fifth graders a kid-friendly version of the "code" adopted in 1942 (www.menc.org/guides/patriotic/reprise.pdf) and how it suggests the national anthem always be performed in a way that everyone can sing along. That leads to great discussion about how it is often performed today.

■ I have introduced a theme with the national anthem, and the students like it very much. Sometimes, I play the anthem as it is played at a baseball game and follow it with "Take Me Out to the Ball Game." Another time, I have the students sing "I Love the United States" and follow with the national anthem. This comes after

A Teacher's Story

I recently taught the national anthem to all of my fourth graders and was pleasantly surprised to find that I did not meet with too much resistance. I played a recording and asked if anyone could identify it. I told them how most Americans don't know the song or think it is too hard, and I even shared with the students how people have tried to change our national anthem because "The Star-Spangled Banner" is challenging. We talked about what made it challenging and how it really isn't too hard for people to sing if they use their head voices, sing with good posture, etc. (all of the things they are learning at school). Then, I taught half of the song. The next week, I taught the rest of the song. We reviewed it in subsequent class sessions. Eventually, they could sing it from memory.

Most of my kids recognized the melody but had the words slightly messed up and struggled with the high part. After a small amount of time in class, they begin to sound good, sing the correct words, and even have an understanding of what the words mean. I spent the first few minutes of each class doing this (less than ten minutes in the first class for background and the first half of the song, five to ten minutes in the next class to finish learning the song, and a couple of minutes reviewing/singing from memory at the beginning of class after that), so it didn't take a huge chunk of my time.

I think it is so important for kids to learn to sing this song, and I was pleased at the response (and sound) from my kids. Of course, there were a few kids who started to act silly as we sang, but I quickly addressed their behavior by mentioning that it was disrespectful to our country to make fun of the national anthem. That was all it took to stop the silliness, and it really did not occur often. Most of my kids wanted to learn the song and were pleased with themselves for doing such a good job, knowing that the public views it as a challenging thing to sing. One big draw to learn it was so that they would know how to do something that their parents probably didn't know how to do. They could go and teach their parents how to sing the song. And, they would know it when it was played at sporting events and ceremonies.

—Ann Holland Hughes
Brooks Museum Magnet Elementary School
Raleigh, NC

I am sure that the students feel comfortable singing all the difficult parts of the anthem and we have analyzed it for form and history. My students feel very strongly about singing the national anthem in a proper manner.

■ We start our unit on the national anthem slowly by listening to it. I ask them if they have ever heard it before. Many children remember hearing it before a game. Then we talk about the proper etiquette of standing and putting our hand on our heart whenever we hear it. We talk about how the baseball players take their hats off and place their hat by their heart. I drill two to four lines per class, going over and over the words and letting them hear the song in full. I also pair it with "Take Me Out to the Ball Game" so that we can do a slow, serious song ("The Star-Spangled Banner") with a fun song (Teresa Jennings's version of "Take Me Out to the Ball Game") with movement and acting. This works well since it is still baseball season in the fall. In the spring, we sing it again before we sing the baseball song because it is baseball season again. Even if the students cannot switch registers yet, perfection of the melody can come later. But the words and the love for their country should be instilled in their little hearts right from the beginning.

■ We read an article by former Senator Andrew Jacobs of Indiana published in *Parade* magazine in November 1988 titled "Should We Change Our National Anthem?" Senator Jacobs gives reasons why he and many other Americans think that our national anthem should be changed to "America the Beautiful." The article is dated, but the argument is timeless. The students then conduct a Socratic seminar to the statement, "I think our national anthem should be ___________ because ..." During the next class period, I debrief the students, playing both sides to bring out thoughtful responses. I never give my personal opinion, but most students think I prefer "America the Beautiful" because I often have to defend that song, because they say, "We've *always* had the Banner!" After this unit, which usually takes four forty-minute class periods, my students have a much better understanding of our national anthem and other patriotic music.

■ A couple of years ago, I bought the paperback book *The Star-Spangled Banner* (ISBN: 0-439-40767-2) by Scholastic. Each page is a single phrase of the anthem accompanied by beautiful photographs of the American flag. Photos are of children in red, white, and blue, marching in a parade, a baseball game, the military, a farmer painting the flag on the roof of his barn, and many more. I was quite surprised at the children's reaction to the pictures. The very first time I get the book out, they oooh and aaahhh and catch their breath every time I turn the page. My students love the anthem because they love the book.

■ I created what I called a patriotic packet of about eight to ten songs including the "Big Three" ("Star-Spangled Banner," "America," and "America the Beautiful") plus "God Bless America," "Battle Hymn of the Republic," "Yankee Doodle," etc. These were available for the students to use to eventually commit them to memory.

PUTTING IT IN CONTEXT

Connections with History

Many music teachers have found that patriotic music is more interesting and relevant if students understand the story behind the song. The words of "The Star-Spangled Banner" make more sense—and perhaps become easier to remember—when students know the story of Francis Scott Key looking at the flag at Fort McHenry during the War of 1812. The national anthem and other patriotic songs also give teachers an opportunity to connect their music lessons with social studies lessons, perhaps working in concert with social studies teachers.

Music teachers have used a variety of techniques and presented many different facts to make the words of the songs come alive.

■ To help students remember the words and show enthusiasm when singing the music, explain it. "Yankee Doodle" was repressed at one time. The national anthem was written by a prisoner. If the children have a story they can relate the music to, they will remember it easier. Try acting out the events that go with the songs to get children excited about it.

■ I have found it extremely helpful to teach the history behind the national anthem for the kids to really "get" the respect with which it is meant to be sung. We talk about the fact that it was actually originally a poem and not a song. I even found a copy of the original in our school library to show them. We talk about the way the words of the poem were added to an old English song (often sung in bars).

■ When teaching "The Star-Spangled Banner," I talk to my middle school students about English Lt. Henry Shrapnel's bombs. This gives them a idea what those bombs really were and the potential devastation to ships and men.

■ One of the most effective ways I've found to teach "The Star-Spangled Banner" in kindergarten to second grade is to dramatize the story. One side of class is British, and the other is American. They love to produce sound effects for the bomb bursting.

■ During the early part of March as part of Music In Our Schools Month, I'll have a PSA made on (or near) March 3, the day "The Star-Spangled Banner" was made our official national anthem. A student gives a brief history of the national anthem.

■ I have a history lesson when teaching the national anthem to my high school choir so that the students can capture the emotion of what the battle must have been like as rockets and bombs lit the night sky revealing ever so briefly that the flag was still there. The discussion concludes as I ask my students the same question that Francis Scott Key asks in the lyrics: Does the flag still wave? Is what they fought for still in place today? Are you still willing to sacrifice as they did to have a land for the free and the brave?

■ In one third-grade class, I started the lesson on "The Star-Spangled Banner" by playing a card game with the class. I told them that I was going to turn over each card in a deck, and if a heart appeared at the end, they would go outside for recess that day; if not, no more recess for the year! I began by turning over each card slowly and dramatically, then sometimes turned two or three at once, then slowly again. Most students were taking the game very seriously. Before the last card, I stopped and asked them what they were thinking at the moment. Then without turning over the last card, I explained that Francis Scott Key was a prisoner on a boat in Baltimore Harbor in 1814, watching to see if "our flag was still there" by watching through the "bombs bursting in air," giving off the "rockets' red glare." (It's always interesting to watch the faces of the students who realize I'm quoting the national anthem!) We then looked at the words and did a dramatic reading of the poetry. (I never turned over the last card in my game—although some cried "no fair!")

■ The students imagine they too are out on a boat off the harbor and see Fort McHenry being attacked in battle. The students imagine they are looking as hard as they can for the American flag to still be waving at Fort McHenry throughout the night—why? That serves as the sign that we are "still free" (the fort has not been successfully captured).

■ I wrote a short two-person play dramatizing the events of the day Francis Scott Key wrote his famous poem. The drama teacher and I did it once before for the staff of the school (many said they finally understood the song!), and now we want to film it for the student body to see.

■ We researched the origins of the melody in the Anacreon society and the several versions of lyrics that Francis Scott Key wrote using the Anacreon melody. (He wrote one set of lyrics in response to a naval victory over pirates!)

■ Annually, I start fourth-grade music with "The Star-Spangled Banner" because it is credited with being written on September 14, 1814. We subtract that date from this year's date to find out the age of the song. I show the video *Our Heritage of American Patriotic Songs* to enable my students to understand the historical setting of the song. While

A Teacher's Story

I have used a wonderful cross-curricular approach to patriotic music in my school. I have developed a patriotic music curriculum in fifth-grade general music in the middle school where I teach. I work with the classroom teachers and follow the fifth-grade social studies curriculum throughout the year. As the students learn about the Revolutionary War, Civil War, intercontinental railroad, WWI, and so on, I teach them about the history of the songs of the time. We sing the songs, march, play instruments, and role-play.

Each time we learn about the songs, I hand out a page that I have prepared, briefly describing the history and important facts about each song. I include the lyrics and pictures of American symbols for the students to color. I play various recordings of the songs while the students work. The students hand in the pages which I keep throughout the year. At the end of the school year, the students design a cover for their patriotic songbook with our art teacher, and we put the songs together in a book.

In the weeks leading up to Memorial Day, I run an essay contest titled "What Patriotic Music Means to Me" and decorate a bulletin board in the hallway with a large plastic flag and stars to display the winning essays. Students must include personal experiences that involve patriotic music and why they think patriotic music is important. I give out medals for the winning essays and call the local newspaper to have their pictures taken. I ask the English teachers to help judge the essays. This program creates a lot of interest in patriotic music for the students.

My next addition to the program that I am working on is putting together an assembly at the end of the year around Flag Day as an opportunity for each homeroom to perform a patriotic song and a brief skit depicting the history behind the song.

—Lisa Moriarty
Cornwall Central Middle School
Monroe, New York

watching the video, they respond to a worksheet that correlates with the video. One time we sing the *entire* "Star-Spangled Banner" because few adults realize there is more than one verse. Then they have to be able to write the words to the first verse of "The Star-Spangled Banner" as a test. Bonus questions focus on the historical background. I tell them that if they ever win a gold medal at the Olympics and stand with the national anthem being performed in their honor, I expect them to be able to sing it!

■ Each year, I have a four-week unit of study with my fifth graders on the national anthem. (I use part of each forty-five-minute music period.) I begin by having them sing the song with the music, if needed. (Most of them do need to use the music.) I also tell them the story of what was happening in history at that time, including information about the battle at Fort McHenry, using literature I got at the fort. I go over certain vocabulary words and definitions that I think they might not know. I use other patriotic songs at the same time and tell them the story behind those as well. I use the Smithsonian's Web site on the national anthem. I prepare questions, and the students go to the school computer lab to search for the answers, like a scavenger hunt. I also play games with questions on the song's words, vocabulary, and history. In the final week, they take a written test.

■ I teach "America" to my first graders. We read it off a large poster and talk about the form and the words … like what fathers the words speak of.

■ We reenact the events surround the writing of the poem. I am blessed to have a balcony outside my room that becomes Fort McHenry during our work. The students pretend to keep watch and, when we all are looking to see it, the school flag pole is in sight!

■ We measured the dimensions of the flag at Fort McHenry using a ball of string, marked at the corners. We went into gym and marked it out on the gym floor, and it was a full half-court big.

■ I show students a picture of the flag that at the Smithsonian that is now being restored. We talk about the pieces that were cut off the flag and why.

■ We studied the meaning of the words very closely. We compared it to the French, British, and Canadian anthems and found that our anthem differs mostly because it is two questions and a statement. Don't get bogged down in the other three verses—some of it is impossible for modern minds to make sense of.

■ Print out a copy of the copy in Francis Scott Key's handwriting. The kids think it's fascinating. And don't forget to get pictures of the actual Star-Spangled Banner currently undergoing restoration at the Smithsonian.

■ Every year, we study "America the Beautiful" in sixth grade. We go over what the words mean—amazingly, most kids do not always know "amber," "alabaster," etc. They are required to do a project to illustrate "America the Beautiful"—they can do it with a partner if they choose. They must show spacious skies, amber waves of grain, purple mountain majesties, fruited plain, sea to shining sea, and alabaster cities. Any extras are extra credit. They must have the title and who wrote the words.

■ This year I offered a prize to any student who would be willing to give a summary of what the lyrics of "The Star-Spangled Banner" mean in plain English (especially important for our English language learners). I had a taker, and it was a wonderful summary everyone could understand.

GETTING IT DOWN

Learning the Words

Even students who understand the words of the great patriotic songs may find it hard to remember them. Teachers use games, puzzles, hand motions, and different kinds of drills to help students remember the words of the great patriotic songs. Many teachers work especially hard on helping students memorize the national anthem so that they will be able to sing proudly at sports and community events.

■ When I reluctantly found myself teaching junior high general music twenty years ago, my initial lessons were designed to get the students involved using songs that they would know ("The Star-Spangled Banner," "America," "America the Beautiful," "Happy Birthday," etc.). The result was not successful, and I was very frustrated that there was no singing going on. Finally, after several attempts, a brave soul raised his hand and said, "It isn't that we are refusing to sing, we don't know the words!" That's when I realized that they might be able to sing if the songs were thoroughly taught and they were expected to learn them. From that day on, learning the words to patriotic songs or "songs that all Americans should know," as I would call them, became a significant portion of our general music curriculum.

■ Even though most students insist they know the words, I have them written out with marker in big, readable letters on four posters, each numbered and posted right on the wall next to the flag in our room (right by the flag so no one will notice if students are reading the words while singing). Each week during a four-week period, we take a numbered section of the words and talk about what it means, thinking of it more like a story than a song.

■ I teach in a private elementary school, and every Friday at the beginning of assembly we sing the national anthem. This can be quite a challenge to kindergartners! But I have a photocopyable book that breaks the first verse down phrase by phrase with an accompanying picture to color. I see my children every day for music, so every day we learn a few more words of the song. At the end of the week, the students take their books with them to assembly and sing for the school. During this week, we formally learn the song and discuss the meaning of the words in a way they can understand. I also share children's books about the national anthem. While they color their pictures, I sing or play the song so they have more opportunities to hear it.

■ After enough practice, I give students a fill-in-the-blank paper with missing words from the first verse of "The Star-Spangled Banner." I grade these and have them sing with their papers again, noting the words that they couldn't remember or put in wrong. I enjoy the humor that I find and share it with the older groups. "Donzerly" is a strange new word that appears early in the song (immediately preceding "light"). This year I got a new one: the "rammed parts" that we watched o'er.

■ I start my choir classes every year with the national anthem. With my middle school kids, I teach them the words phrase by phrase and go over the meaning in the lines. I teach the song by rote since it's the beginning of the year and I want them to be able to achieve some success right away. After they've learned the first verse, we examine the other three verses and point out that the first verse is just the beginning of the story. I have had them rewrite the first verse so that it makes sense in their own language and they understand what it means by applying that knowledge.

■ I used to teach "The Star-Spangled Banner" to my first graders every year in February. I would teach the song in four parts—backwards. Most of them could remember the last part of the song from ball games. The next week, I would teach the action part: "rockets' red glare." For the "whose broad stripes" part, we would talk about the flag—its stripes and stars. Finally, we would learn the first part. At the end of each lesson, we would sing the part we had just learned. I would give a "Star-Spangled" award (sticker with flag on it) to the boy or girl who stood the straightest and sang the best. It was surprising the number of times second-grade students would ask to sing "The Star-Spangled Banner."

■ We play the "beach ball" game to make learning the words of "The Star-Spangled Banner" fun. To play, we pass around a beach ball while standing in a circle. The first person says the first word of the song and then each person says the next word in the song as they get the ball. At the beginning of the year, we see how far we get in the song before making a mistake. As the year goes along, it becomes an elimination game—if you make a mistake, you're out! The winner sometimes receives an American flag sticker or gets to choose an instrument to play. It's an easy game for a substitute teacher to use as well!

■ I printed and laminated postcard-size word cards with red, white, and blue borders and patriotic clip art. I broke the song into phrases and made enough card sets for a class to work in groups of two or three to arrange the cards in the proper order. I had originally planned to use it in late second grade and for fall review in third, but I found that first graders could use them late in the year, too. Not all of them could read all the words, but they helped each other and were generally all successful the first time.

■ For third, fourth, and fifth grade, I have the words written out in short phrases laminated on 8" by 10" poster paper. I pass them out to fifteen students and let the students put them in order—without saying a word. We look at it phrase by phrase—a correct phrase gets a thumbs up. If the students get to a phrase that is out of order, the remaining classmates show thumbs to the side. I can see them singing it in their heads as we go along, so they are thinking.

■ One practice strategy I have used is to fragment the text into groups of two or three words on a strip of construction paper and divide the song among the students. Each student holds a fragment and as a class we attempt to assemble the song correctly. As we repeat this activity, we should get faster.

■ One thing we have done in class that really gets the students excited and searching their minds and memories for the next word is what I call "The Lyrics Game." We use this game with all of our songs that we will perform throughout the year. The students are divided into two equal teams. The first student on Team One says the first word ("Oh"), then the second student must come up with the second word ("say"), etc. Team members continue reciting the lyrics in this way until they make a mistake. When a team misses, they rotate (person #1 moves to the end of the line), and the other team takes a turn. Students need to listen to their own team so that they will be ready when their turn comes, and they need to listen to the opposing team so they can raise their hands when someone misses! Also, sometimes listening to the other team helps them to learn a word they got stuck on in an earlier turn. There really isn't any scoring—the kids get all excited trying to get through to the end and don't seem to care who "wins."

■ I use the following patriotic puzzles activity to help students learn patriotic songs.

1. Write each phrase of the patriotic songs on a sentence strip. (I use different colors to help keep them organized.)
2. Introduce a new song by dividing the class into groups according to the number of phrases in the song.
3. Give one phrase to each group.
4. Each group reads its phrase to the other groups.
5. The class talks about new vocabulary and the meaning of the words.
6. Everyone listens to the song.
7. Ask groups to put the song back together in a pocket chart.
8. Listen again to check for correct order of the phrases. Repeat if necessary.
9. Sing together.

After introducing about five songs, I vary the activity by giving each group a whole song to place in order in the pocket chart for the class to sing. We rotate the songs among the groups, sing in groups, and do whatever else we think of that sounds fun. Pretty soon students are asking me for copies of the song so they can cut them apart and have their own personal patriotic puzzles. I appreciate the literacy aspect since reading is such a major focus at my school.

■ Last year I taught every grade, including kindergarten, "The Star-Spangled Banner" using sign language to help them to remember the words. I have students in my class who have just entered the United States. I can't tell you how touched I was when they sang the song for the first time with such expression!

■ I had my kindergarten and first-grade students make up motions for each line. They came up with some unique ones. Whenever they forgot a line, I just had to do their special motion and they remembered the line. It made the song their own. We eventually were able to sing it without the motions. I told them to internalize the motions and play them over with the video camera of their mind. It worked!

■ Every year I teach "The Star-Spangled Banner" to my fifth graders (and fourth if we have combination classes). I require that they have at least 80 percent of the words memorized by themselves before they leave school in the spring. This way I feel they are fully capable of singing the national anthem at ball games and other events. I have my students sing it alone to me at the piano. They can speak it or write it if they wish, but I let them know that it is much easier if they sing it because the melody will help them remember.

■ I grew up in small farm and railroad town where every concert and all community events began with "The Star-Spangled Banner." I have continued the tradition, without fail, in all of my thirty years of programs. I annually challenge our fifth graders to memorize the national anthem. Each student who does so receives a certificate of completion at the end of the

A Teacher's Story

I teach elementary general music as well as high school vocal music in Chesterfield Township near New Baltimore, Michigan. When I began teaching, I made it a priority to teach the words and music of the national anthem each year to second- and third-grade students and review them regularly with the fourth- and fifth-grade students. I usually start by reading a book about when Francis Scott Key was inspired to write the words. I have the children act out parts of the story so they understand the story more completely. Through this activity I am able to teach the meaning of words like "hailed," "twilight," "gleaming," and "rampart."

I also have coloring pages for each line of the song that form into a book when the students are done coloring. Each day for two weeks, I begin the class by singing a line from the song. Then the students begin to color the pages. While they are coloring the pages, I play different versions of "The Star-Spangled Banner" as well as other patriotic music.

After they've completed their booklets, I listen to each child sing the song individually at the piano. This is done in a very nonthreatening way. The students are busy coloring or reading while I sing with each individual student. The last step is to encourage the students to read or sing the song to at least two people outside school.

The fourth- and fifth-grade students perform the national anthem as part of their music program each year. Since the students learn the words and melody in second and third grade, I can begin to teach good vocal technique and musical phrasing in fourth and fifth grade. I also use this song to teach head voice and chest voice to my older elementary students. This song is perfect for this concept because it is so high. It is very difficult to carry your chest voice up into the higher notes. They truly begin to understand the vocal techniques that are necessary for a quality choral sound. Every year the high school choirs learn to sing the national anthem for various community performances.

—Deborah Root
Sugarbush Elementary and Anchor Bay High School
Chesterfield, MI

year awards banquet. The kids are given the option of reciting the lyrics, singing the lyrics, or writing them from memory. (I do not grade for spelling in the written option.) It is important to note that the kids say or sing the lyrics to me "up close and personal," out of the range of their peers' ears. Three minor errors (e.g., "at the twilight's last streaming" instead of "gleaming") or one major error (the most common is dropping "Whose broad stripes and bright stars" and going directly to "And the rockets' red glare") negates the effort for the day. Students are allowed to try once daily throughout the third nine weeks. They can see me before and after school, during lunch, or at the end of music class. Some kids search me out. Others … well, I have to hunt 'em down a few times. After that, they must take the initiative to get the job done.

Singing with Pride

Learning the Music

Most music teachers would probably agree that "The Star-Spangled Banner" is not an easy song to sing. The high notes, long phrases, and obscure words can make this song especially challenging for young singers. Teachers have found ways to meet the challenge by focusing on the vocal skills needed, providing models for students to listen to, and offering lots of opportunities for students to sing the song in class.

■ As far as skill, you simply have to stick to your standards for any singing. Patriotic songs are no more or less important to sing with the best singing voice than any other songs.

■ I usually do not attempt "The Star-Spangled Banner" until the second grade as I find that the range is just too much for younger children.

■ It is fruitless to try to sing the national anthem unless the students understand their head voice and chest voice ranges and have had years of practice getting in and out of these extremes. Not all of my fourth graders can do it. All of them are willing and proud to try. We can ask no more. What's more, many of them can sing it more accurately than their parents can. That is an accomplishment in itself.

■ If we don't tell the students that the national anthem is difficult, they won't think it is. Most book series have the song in the key of A-flat. This key seems to work the best. If students have trouble getting down to the A-flat, I just tell them to sing it with a very relaxed jaw and throat and to sing it softly. I help them sing complete phrases by explaining the meaning in the words. For example, "For the land [breath] of the free" does not make any literal sense. I say, "surely you can sing more than three words without taking a breath. Just sail up there. Think about being free." Then I demonstrate singing the whole phrase from "and the land of the free and the home of the brave" and say, "If I can do that, then surely you can sing 'and the land of the free' without taking a breath." Then the students try it and find out that they can.

■ I compare athletes to singers and tell them that exercising the voice is like lifting weights. They have to exercise their voice to reach the notes.

■ I almost always teach "The Star-Spangled Banner" in fifth grade. Since it has such a large range, it is risky to teach it earlier. This year some of my fifth-grade students asked to do it early in the year because they were learning to sign it in their classroom. I told them I would love to do it, but they would need to teach me to sign it along the way so the other two classes could learn the signing for our concert. They loved the challenge of teaching me to sign. We worked on one phrase at a time, their goal being to match the pitches, mine to learn the signing well enough to teach the other classes. In the process, we were both winners.

■ I sing it in A-flat, which puts the highest note at a high E-flat. This is well within the appropriate singing range for fifth graders, although the beginning is a bit low. We focus on good singing posture, dropping the jaw, not "turtle-necking" the high notes, but rather imagining that the sound comes out of the top of the head, rather like a whale's blowhole.

■ I have found that on "and the rockets' red glare," it is much easier for many of my students to sing the lower harmony (a third below the melody) so they don't strain their voices.

■ The range of notes encompasses three vocal registers. This is a lot to expect from singers. They must be trained and skilled in using their voice in all three registers, and they need to know which part of the song uses which register. A-flat seems to be the favorite key; however, with children who can soar in their upper registers, B-flat is also a good key.

■ Before singing "The Star-Spangled Banner," I sing the original "To Anacreon in Heaven" for the class. It's interesting to watch the reactions of the students who realize they know the tune. When students are learning the song (or relearning it), I begin with the last phrase, having the class sing it through while attempting to avoid the usual big breath between "star-spangled" and "banner yet wave." They really surprise themselves when they can sing it in one breath. (I've done this with all age groups, from the youngest to high school.) We work on producing a good head tone, and singing *softly*, in the key of A-flat.

■ On "favorites day," the national anthem is probably the most requested song. I usually drop the key a step or two and encourage the boys to sing in their head voices, especially on the high part. At first, some kids laughed and said they sounded like girls. I compare them to some of the most famous pop singers that sing in their head voices and tell the kids, "Laugh if you want—those singers are laughing all the way to the bank."

■ I make sure to give credit with my students both to Francis Scott Key for the words *and* to John Stafford Smith for the music.

■ A good activity is to match melodic lines with lyrics activity. Students have to read a line from the melody to themselves, think about how it would sound, then match it to the correct lyrics.

■ At times I give them a piece of the song. (I have chopped the song into four parts and numbered them.) Each child sings his or her part then they trade parts and sing again. This is kind of nice to get them singing parts and listening to others.

■ I have students count how many times they hear *sol-mi-do* in one verse of "The Star-Spangled Banner." Then I have them conduct, in three, along with the song, being sure to place stressed words on the down beat.

■ We listen to a tape I have of "The Star-Spangled Banner" and how it sounded in 1814.

■ We listen to many various recordings of this song. One very interesting version is by Bela Fleck and the Flecktones done on the banjo.

■ Often I have students who want to sing patriotic songs with their own style or flair. I discuss what is acceptable with the style of these songs versus a pop tune. I will give an example of an "overembellished" rendition of the national anthem versus a more acceptable rendition that allows the students to see the difference. This can also be done with recordings of the national anthem sung by soloists and choirs. I believe it is really important that our students understand the stylistic nature and the emotional impact of patriotic music when performing and listening to it.

■ Older elementary students have thought of patriotic songs as "old songs," so I motivated them to sing it by providing videos of popular musicians who have been chosen to sing it. I showed the video of Whitney Houston singing it at the Super Bowl. After seeing her sing it, they had more of a desire to learn it.

■ I have heard many arrangements sung by many singers and decided to do something original. I wrote my own four-part, with an occasional fifth part, arrangement to the national anthem, which is sung by my seventh- and eighth-grade chorus.

■ I wrote the arrangement that we use. It is an a capella arrangement that features the men in three-part harmony during "And the rockets' red glare, the bombs bursting in air." My guys take such pride each year in making sure that they "nail" that four-measure section.

■ After the students are basically familiar with the melody and words, I bring out the instruments—cymbals and drums. I have three or four students using the instruments. As we sing, I direct the instrumentalists to play at certain times in the anthem. For example, a clashing of cymbals or drums follows the words "O, say can you see" (CLASH), "rockets' red glare" (CLASH), and "bombs bursting in air" (CLASH). Then toward the end, there are many "clashes" on the beat. This way, the students get to sing it many times (so all can get a turn with the instruments) without getting bored.

■ In second grade, I use "The Star-Spangled Banner" to teach students about phrases. After each phrase of the song, they play finger cymbals or an instrument of their choice. For example, "O say, can you see by the dawn's early light" (ching), "What so proudly we hailed at the twilight's last gleaming" (ching), etc.

■ I include "The Star-Spangled Banner" as a three-meter song in my meter unit, having some students play finger cymbals on the strong beat. In fourth or fifth grade, I use metallophone notes (chord roots) on the strong beat, in the key of B-flat, which does take them up to a high F, but I really praise them for being able to sing in their light voice that high. Sometimes I also have one student conduct with a baton, after we have practiced conducting in three.

■ I use the national anthem almost every day as an ending portion of my vocal warm-up exercises. I can use it to extend students' vocal ranges and teach breath management, phrasing, and diction. We often "mess around" with the national anthem by singing it staccato/legato in alternate phrases (great for connecting the breath energy and diaphragm). We sing it with various dynamic levels, too, and often try to sing it with differing vocal styles (British opera singers, old ladies with wobbly vibratos, various ages of schoolchildren, etc.) to expand students' knowledge of what their voices can do.

■ I use the national anthem as a weekly exercise in musical dynamics. I conduct with varying tempo, ritardando, crescendo, decrescendo, use of articulation, etc., so they will learn to "follow the stick" and play more musically. The chorus sings in two parts and also plays "follow the conductor" as I start and stop, crescendo, etc. They have fun with it and develop a sense of a patriotic identity.

A Teacher's Story

I love the old, standard version of the national anthem and have taught it to my students in each of my six years of teaching. I try to teach all of my students each of the parts, SATB. We start with the bass, my favorite part. My students love being able to sing more than one part. Some are able to sing all four. They love that. The girls so far have been easier to assemble as an all-female group. I hope to get an all-male group together one of these days.

We share it a cappella with the student body at home basketball games in small ensembles as the ROTC presents the colors. They are so proud of themselves that they can sing it beautifully and confidently without my leadership. A student invariably discovers that he or she can lead from the group, and the rest learn that they can follow! Sometimes a former student has come from the crowd and volunteered to fill a gap in a part.

We use it to further our understanding of the diatonic scale, solfège and even chord spelling. We have done a little group "arranging" as well. My goal this year is to learn and teach more about its origin and historical impact.

—Sylvia B. Lowry
North Surry High School
Mount Airy, NC

■ "The Star-Spangled Banner" sometimes poses a certain level of difficulty to younger grades. However, there are ways to teach it:

1. Learn two phrases at a time—repeat until they can sing in tune with proper words.
2. Rhythm. It is written in 3/4 time, just like a lullaby. Young children get used to it very fast.
3. Stress the importance of what the song stands for.
4. Tell the story of Francis Scott Key—makes it more interesting with a visual association.
5. Since the range (tessatura) of the piece is wide, it is a perfect song for teaching vocal techniques. The young children *can* tell the difference between chest tones versus head voice.
6. I make it a requirement for my choirs to learn it.
7. I respect certain religions that prohibit a handful of students from participating.
8. Interpretation is important—since it is a patriotic song representing our country. It leads to facial expressions, proper hand gesture (right hand over left chest), head held high with confidence.
9. Starting from third grade on, the history of the anthem should be taught, including the number of verses.
10. Patriotism and nationalism are the two hidden ingredients in learning this piece. Our children need to care about our country.
11. Singing it a capella is not so difficult if every rehearsal starts with it as a warm-up.
12. Phrasing is extremely important. One breath per two phrases maximum. Breath control is the basis of good vocal technique.

Creating Rituals

Long-Range Plans and Schoolwide Participation

Patriotic music can provide schools with an opportunity to establish schoolwide rituals for assemblies, morning announcements, and other events. These rituals give many students a reason to learn the music and offer them places to sing and hear the music they are learning. Many music teachers make patriotic songs a vital part of their curriculum, developing a sequential program that includes specific patriotic songs or musical skills at each grade level. Such programs can make patriotic music and patriotism part of a school's culture and identity.

■ Annually, I have an all-school "Music in Our Schools Day" celebration. Every fifth year (because first through fifth grades participate), I use the theme of patriotic songs so that all my students learn to sing the most common patriotic songs.

■ I start the year with the typical warm-ups and games, then I move directly into our patriotic unit. All students learn a patriotic song, memorized for a voice test later on in the year. Sixth graders learn one verse of "America." Seventh graders learn three verses of "This Land Is Your Land." (This song lends itself to the changing voices in the boys—you can put it in the key of G and have them sing in the middle-C range.) Eighth graders learn three verses of "America the Beautiful."

■ I use patriotic music as a warm-up song for my K–5 students. I choose songs based on form, range, and lyrics appropriate for each grade. Here's a list of what I use for each grade:

K: "Sing Out for Your Country"
1: "Yankee Doodle," "The Flag Goes By, Hats Off"
2: "You're a Grand Old Flag," "This is My Country"
3: "America" (My Country 'Tis of Thee), "Home on the Range"
4: "God Bless America," "Yankee Doodle Dandy"
5: "America the Beautiful," "The Star-Spangled Banner," "Lift Every Voice and Sing," "50 Nifty United States"

■ I teach my fifth graders the national anthem each year. From kindergarten through fifth, all my students learn patriotic songs at their grade level. By the time they get to third or fourth grade they ask if they can do "The Star-Spangled Banner." Doing it in the last nine weeks of fifth grade, prior to going on to the middle school, makes it a milestone in their education. It's something they look forward to. They also get to sing it for their final elementary concert in late May, which is almost like a graduation of sorts.

■ I have my students sing one of three patriotic songs at the beginning of each music class. Kindergarten and first grades sing "America." I add "America the Beautiful" to the repertoire in second grade and "The Star-Spangled Banner" in third grade.

■ I begin the year reviewing the songs learned from the previous year like "America, the Beautiful," etc. We reread the books I have that match song titles. Of course, our kindergartners begin from scratch. I then begin to teach the words. I have created hand motions for the words in each song. Some of the hand motions are actually sign language. We also hold regularly scheduled monthly assemblies where many patriotic songs are learned—including the new ones from *Music K–8* like "Lights of Freedom," "Put Your Hand over Your Heart," "I Love My Country," etc.

■ Each year the students in my K–8 school work to learn "The Star-Spangled Banner" in a variety of ways, depending on the age group. The song is introduced to the primary students in kindergarten to third grade. In fourth grade, we introduce verses two and three to the students. In fifth grade, the students prepare a "Star-Spangled Banner" book, using the computer lab for five sessions. The students prepare illustrations to accompany the words of the song, read articles on the history of the flag and the song, and type the words to all of the verses. All of these items are included in their booklets before they are bound and displayed in the hallway. Next year, the sixth graders will be preparing a PowerPoint presentation, using our new SMART Board, to present a multimedia presentation on the Grandparents Day performance, while the chorus sings the song.

■ I teach general music for third through sixth grade. Between fourth and fifth grades, the students move to a different school. Their "final exam" in the fourth grade is to be able to sing the national anthem. We begin teaching their full range even in kindergarten. In the third grade, we reinforce head voice and chest voice and explore their high range frequently with siren noises, head-voice speech, and songs with wide ranges. Starting in fourth grade, we study the full story of Francis Scott Key and the writing of the poem. It is a great tale, worthy of Hollywood. By the middle of fourth grade, the students are pleased and proud to be able to sing a song considered so difficult. I bring out the karaoke machine, and they are all allowed to take a turn singing part of the anthem. Their "final exam" is to sing "The Star-Spangled Banner" for the whole school (as a group, of course) when the flag is lowered the last two minutes of the school year.

■ The first Friday of each month at our school is "Red, White, and Blue Day." We have a class or group of students perform the national anthem on our morning announcements that day. This is a big motivator for them to learn it. My students know that if their class was following directions well and they did their best while learning the national anthem, they will get a chance to sing it on our morning announcements.

■ In our elementary school, we sing the national anthem at our flag assemblies each month. In September, I always start the year singing the patriotic songs that are in the students' music textbooks. We always start learning "The Star-Spangled Banner" in the third grade, although everyone has been hearing it sung by the other students for several years. By the time the students are in fifth grade, they are singing all the verses. The kids at our school love to sing it, and many can't wait to find it in their books in third grade. Often, the other teachers complain about how hard it is to sing, but not the students. We sing it a capella most of the time, so I really get to hear which students still need more work on singing in their upper register voices and matching pitch.

■ At my school, we do our morning announcements through a closed-circuit television broadcast. Upon my starting work at that school three years ago, I was assigned as one of the "producers" of the show. (Two teachers share the responsibility.) In addition to the regular morning activities, I added a patriotic song last year. We use PowerPoint to put messages up on the screen like "Coming up next," so I created a PowerPoint presentation with the words to "The Star-Spangled Banner," "America," and "America the Beautiful." We rotate the songs every month or so. I uploaded recordings of the pieces onto the computer and as the song plays, the words appear on their television screens. This has helped clear up most of the mis-singing of lyrics to these songs, and I am proud to say that *every* child (and teacher) at my school knows the national anthem, "America" (two verses even!), and "America the Beautiful"!

■ At our school, we take one patriotic song per six weeks and have children sing it over the intercom during morning announcements. They take turns introducing themselves and sing their hearts out for the chance to be heard.

■ At my school, we sing both "The Star-Spangled Banner" and the black national anthem ("Lift Every Voice and Sing") for all assemblies. You can also post the lyrics on the wall, doors, etc., in the music room and in the auditorium/cafetorium. I have also had members from the Portland Opera, school staff, and teachers to sing anthems for our assemblies. I feel confident that at least 80–90 percent of our students can sing the anthems mentioned above. We take pride in singing the anthems and offer much respect.

■ We have assembly *every* day. Each assembly begins with the Pledge of Allegiance and a patriotic song. Each nine weeks, we sing a different patriotic song. The national anthem is saved for the last nine weeks. The first part of each nine weeks, a transparency with words to the song is shown on the stage screen. After that, students must sing without that help. I teach an age-appropriate lesson each nine weeks for each song. I give fourth

A Teacher's Story

I am the choral director at Avon Grove High School in West Grove, Pennsylvania. When I came there fourteen years ago, there was no choral program at all, so one of my goals became to teach the national anthem and the school's alma mater to every singer who entered my choir room! I teach the melody, four-part harmony, different arrangements, etc.

I pointed out to the students how badly people sing the national anthem on television, often with the wrong words and terrible arrangements. I teach them to sing it proudly and with enthusiasm. We work on the diction to make the words clear and discuss the meaning of them. Students know that my pet peeve is for someone to take a breath between "Star-Spangled" and "Banner," so we work on the breath control for that phrase so that the students can sing it as a full noun in one breath.

In order to set a goal for the students, I looked for places and events for us to sing the anthem and alma mater. Sometimes the first event of the year is an opening day assembly! We sing both for our homecoming opening ceremony in September or October, so the anthem and alma mater are the first two pieces of music that we learn or review each year. I insist that both be memorized, of course. We learn them both a capella and with accompaniment. We learn them in different combinations of singers, as a whole choir, in quartets, in trios, duets, small ensembles, etc.

During football, basketball, and wrestling seasons, I have students sign up to be the national anthem singers for the home athletic events. All of these performances are done a capella, since they are in the gym or outdoors on a field. At the opening and closing events of each sport, I have the entire Golden Chorale, my top ensemble of twenty-four students, sing the anthem. I have had many coaches compliment me on the way my singers sing the anthem. They have often said that the Avon Grove singers sing the anthem better than any of the other schools in our league. Comments like that make me feel that I have done my job in teaching it!

I have sent trios and quartets to national anthem contests and twice have had a female trio win the honor of singing it at the women's tennis tournament at Villanova University. Next, I would like to have my entire choir sing the anthem at a Phillies or Eagles game. We're working on that one.

Each year in March, during Music In Our Schools Month, we perform a miniconcert in the school lobby as students enter before school. At the end of that concert, we sing the national anthem over the PA system after the Pledge of Allegiance. We have also sung the anthem at the state capitol in Harrisburg when we were invited there during Music In our Schools Month.

One of my singers always performs the anthem to begin our annual talent show right before Christmas break.

To conclude each year, the anthem is the first thing performed at graduation, and the entire senior class sings the alma mater to conclude the ceremony. We accomplish this by making it part of the graduation practices, printing the words in the graduation program so that parents can sing along, and having a strong song leader at the microphone as they sing it. Our band also plays along to make the singing stronger. Singing the alma mater is the very last thing that our students do in their high school careers. Isn't that nice? Graduation begins and ends with the anthem and the alma mater—exactly what the choir students started with on their first day in ninth grade!

High school ends with music, with singing at Avon Grove. Now that's really advocating music in our schools!

—Barbara-Jo Vanderkraats
Avon Grove High School
West Grove, Pennsylvania

and fifth graders a test on words only for each song toward the end of the marking period. Students who make no mistakes receive a certificate. During the final honors assembly, students who received all four certificates get a "USA Award." You may think that testing and rewarding won't help the musicality, but the kids really like getting those awards.

■ Our school district expects students to know the first verse of the national anthem by the end of fourth grade. However, we start learning it in the third grade. For the final concert of the year, students help select the songs we sing. In May 2004, the third-grade students voted to sing the national anthem as one of their selections.

■ To teach my kids the national anthem, I make it one of my "Songs of the Month" very early in the year. I take these songs off the MENC "songs all kids should know" list that has been turned into the *Get America Singing … Again* series.

Taking It to the Streets

Performance Opportunities

Opportunities to perform patriotic songs abound in many communities. Public events ranging from high school football games to Veterans Day celebrations often incorporate patriotic music. By seeking out such performance venues, teachers can give students a reason to learn to sing these songs well while providing valuable positive PR for the school music program.

■ My high school choral students all learn the national anthem as part of their choir classes, and this helps them prepare to audition for solo vocalist opportunities to sing the national anthem at various school events (assemblies, sporting events, special meetings, etc.), as well as helping them to lead the way in singing the song at community events.

■ I start my year teaching the Illinois state song because it is legato singing, and I also teach the national anthem. The high school students must memorize it because I require that the high school choir sing it at least three football games in the season as well as three basketball games, including the county basketball tournament. I also offer extra credit to those who sing it at games as a soloist or in a small ensemble. Making it mandatory for games also helped to get parents to support the program more—the kids like it because they can get into the games free.

■ My chorus students sing the national anthem at football and basketball games at our school. They are motivated to learn to sing the song and excited to audition for small-group "performances." As a group, my eighth graders perform the anthem at an assembly, so they all have a goal to work for.

■ My motivation for them is the opportunity for them to sing the anthem in small groups before our high school's home basketball and football games. This gives them a small-group performance opportunity, creates good PR for my program, and builds a sense of K–12 community in our district.

■ I'm in a large high school choral program with almost four hundred singers. Each year, the Madrigal Singers, the senior ensemble, learn an eight-part arrangement by Hall Johnson (Golden Music Publishers, G138). They perform it at awards night, graduation, and civic events. Also, individual singers and instrumentalists, who study privately and are capable of this range, perform the anthem at sporting events and pep assemblies. They wait for the opportunity; it has become an honor to be selected.

■ My high school choir annually sings "The Star-Spangled Banner" at the homecoming game, and since my first year here we have sung the first and fourth verse, which have become especially pertinent since 9-11. Educating the public to the fact that we are singing two verses is difficult—they always cheer after the first, but we keep going. Maybe someday they will listen to the announcement that says "two verses."

■ I will have the audience sing the national anthem for football games and all other major gatherings instead of using my band or a special guest. I may use a single instrument to sound the starting pitch to get them started.

■ We sometimes include it at the beginning of a concert, asking the audience to sing with us. You wouldn't believe how many kids do *not* know the first verse of our national anthem by heart. Also, many of them *never* sing it because they think it is supposed to be done by a soloist only at the beginning of a ball game. I pitch it a bit lower, in A or G below middle C, so that they can reach the high note without a problem. I encourage the kids to sing along at ball games and special events.

■ Our efforts at learning the anthem lead up to the November 11th Veterans Day ceremony, which is held in a large civic auditorium in town every year. All the seventh- and eighth-grade students in our school are bused to the auditorium for the program. Every other year, my eighth-grade choir sings for the program (alternating with the other middle school choir in town).

■ I made several recordings of my students singing the national anthem for use at our community Little League Park. I have quite a few eighth-grade boys in chorus this year who also play baseball. One recording has one entire mixed chorus singing (about seventy-five singers), another has all the eighth-grade boys on Little League baseball teams (about twenty boys), and another has all the eighth-grade boys on AAU baseball teams (about eight boys). That way, for each kind of game or tournament, the guys can hear themselves singing the national anthem. The players, parents, and siblings pay more attention to the music when they know it might be "their" recording. I'm also hoping this will be a good recruiting tool for younger boys who are potential chorus members, since this particular class of eighth graders has many good athletes who also sing.

■ We planned a field trip for our music students to perform at the Kennedy Space Center. The orchestra and the choir made plans to perform the national anthem. A last-minute thought was to record the students for our school's opening announcements, which usually included the Pledge followed by messages to the student body and faculty concerning the day's events. This is broadcast on closed-circuit TV. To make it more visually appropriate, we planned to perform at the base of the flagpole in front of the school. So viewers could see the flag, we requested permission to lower the flag into a viewable level. Then a second thought came alive. Why not dedicate the rehearsal and taping to the troops overseas? The night before the event, I called local television stations and, lo and behold, our students were featured on the evening news complete with the principal's statement of thanks to the students.

■ This past June, we were invited to be one of the school groups that sang along the route of the running of the Olympic torch through New York City.

■ In November of 2002, I was approached by a parent of a former high school student who was in group sales for the Pittsburgh Pirates. He asked if I would like to bring my fourth-grade chorus down to PNC park and sing the national anthem. I responded with, "Does it have to be just the fourth-grade chorus or can I include any of my students in

A Teacher's Story

Montgomery Bell Academy is a boys' preparatory school (seventh through twelfth grade) in Nashville, Tennessee. My high school chorus prepares a TTBB arrangement of the national anthem each year. (The veteran singers, of course, already know it.) We are asked to sing before football and basketball games.

A wonderful thing happened when our wrestling coach approached *me* and asked if the wrestlers who are in chorus could sing as a small ensemble to open several of the matches. So there they are in their wrestling suits in the center of gym, singing the national anthem, and then proceeding to whup their opponents. (This venture was not at all harmed by the fact that for the past six years we have had at least one All-State Wrestling champ who was a featured soloist in chorus—one soloist was even a four-time state champ!) When this semi-chorus cannot do it, we usually find a soloist from the wrestling team who is also in chorus.

The concept has caught on. The athletic director regularly seeks *me* out to find out who will sing the national anthem each week. We send soloists to state track meets, state swim meets, and baseball games. The opportunities for solo work, even if it is just this one piece, has brought out a lot of courage and confidence in our boys. Also, often the large chorus cannot all make it, and this gives our select small Headmaster Singers a chance to perform. And, if all else fails, we have been known to jury-rig a vocal quartet for the occasion. We even send instrumentalists to open the ball games. I never thought I would say it, but one of our premier violinists even played before a basketball game. I thought "this will never fly," but the whole gymnasium was completely silent for his rendition.

Sometimes my free approach pushes our collective taste a bit far, as when one of our boys who is a rabid country fan decided to do the national anthem à la Clint Black! While not dignified enough for my taste, it is worth it to me to see the guys stepping up, as soloists or in a group.

—Dr. David Cassell
Director of Music
Montgomery Bell Academy
Nashville, Tennessee

kindergarten through fourth grade?" He responded with, "Why sure." So I created a Family Night at the ballpark. For $14 dollars per person, they would receive a ticket to the game, a T-shirt for the singer, and transportation to and from the field.

■ To get my students to learn the anthem, I have built a relationship with our local Major League Baseball team. Every year for the last five years, I have taught the students the anthem and then made arrangements to have them sing it before a baseball game. The kids love the experience, and it is fairly easy. In my case, the team asks that we sell a certain number of tickets in exchange. It is usually not a problem since parents, families, and friends want to see the kids sing at the ballpark. I have kids talking about the experience years later.

Resources

The following books, recordings, and other resources can help teachers use patriotic music in the classroom.

Books for Teachers

■ *Get America Singing … Again* (Milwaukee, WI: Hal Leonard, 1996).

■ *The Music Teacher's Almanac* by Loretta Mitchell (West Nyack, NY: Parker Publishing, 1992).

■ *National Anthems from around the World* (Milwaukee, WI: Hal Leonard, 1996).

Children's Books

■ *America the Beautiful* by Katherine Lee Bates and illustrated by Neil Waldman (New York: Atheneum Books, 1993).

■ *By the Dawn's Early Light: The Story of the Star-Spangled Banner* by Steven Kroll with illustrations by Dan Andreasen (New York: Scholastic, 1994).

■ *Our Flag* by Eleanor Ayer (Brookfield, CT: Millbrook Press, 1992).

■ *The Star-Spangled Banner* illustrated by Peter Spier (New York: Bantam Doubleday, 1973).

■ *The Star-Spangled Banner* (New York: Scholastic, 2002).

Organizations

■ America Sings (www.americasings.org) offers a workshop at its festivals on how to perform "The Star-Spangled Banner" in sign language.

■ The International Barbershop Society (www.spebsqsa.org) has a youth outreach program using patriotic singing for elementary through middle school students.

■ MENC's National Anthem Project Web site (www.thenationalanthemproject.org) offers information on MENC's efforts to help Americans learn—or relearn—the national anthem. The site includes links to the complete lyrics of the anthem and the code for the singing of the anthem.

■ The Smithsonian Institution (http://americanhistory.si.edu/ssb/) offers information on Francis Scott Key and on the restoration of the flag that inspired him to write the "The Star-Spangled Banner." The site includes links to the earliest known manuscript of Key's poem, the words to all four verses, and an audio recording of a nineteenth-century version of the national anthem.

Video and Audio Recordings

First Invasion: The War of 1812 (www.historychannel.com) is a documentary about the War of 1812. It is available in a set with *Save Our History: The Star-Spangled Banner.*

Liberty for All: A Musical Journey from MENC (www.menc.org) is a CD-ROM of live performances by "The President's Own" U.S. Marine Band tracing six eras of American history through song.

Patriotic Songs and Marches from Kimbo Educational (www.kimboed.com) is an audio recording of patriotic songs and marches sung by children.

Save Our History: The Star-Spangled Banner (www.historychannel.com) is a documentary that tells the story of the siege at Fort McHenry and the origin of the national anthem.

Contributors

The following teachers provided ideas used in this book. Although not all suggestions could be used, MENC greatly appreciates the time that each contributor took to share ideas. We thank all participants for being willing to share their success stories and insight.

Curt Abrahamson
Edward H. Allen
Kay Anderson
Jamie Baldwin
Lauren Baker
Nadia Barghouti
Francesca Beahan
Flo Bickel
Elizabeth Brackin
Peggy Breese
Shirley Brockenborough
Ardath Burrer
Cheryl Bredeson
Cindy Buehling
Karen Burdette
Teresa Carroll
David Cassel
Patti Chern
Elaine Clancy
Verna Clark
Cori Copeland
Andrea Cottrill
Steve Cox
Betty Daughtry
Ginny Dawson
Karen Dickhut
Cristen Dimas
Gayle Dirksen
Dorothy Dishman
Paul "Dobbie" Dobson
Susan Dommer
Nancy Duhrkoop
Marsha Etzkorn
Linda Fahlgren
Winn Floyd
Jan Freemore
Paul Gambale
Dena Garrard
Susan Gebren
Jim Gleason
Emanuel Goss
Rose M. Grelis
Marilyn Gunn
Becky Hall
Diane Hamilton
Amelia J. Hannemann
Vicki N. Helms
Chuck Hensley
Marjorie Hildebrandt
Diane Hires
Andrea Hofmeister
Cheryl Huber
Ann Hughes
Margi Jared
Judy Kawalek
Julie Kellum
Todd Lamson
Dianne LaVerne
Mindy LeBlanc
Karen Lee
Nancy Hanna Leong
Rodney Lie
Laura Lofton
Sylvia B. Lowry
Ada Maddox
Jill Mahy
Judith Mank
Jim McBride
Christine McCaffrey
Martha McKie
Fred Meads
Kathleen Milford
Suzanna Miller
Lisa Moriarty
Kelly S. Mott
Jim Mousseau
Darlene Needham
Ruth Novak
Curt Nelson
Michelle Olson
Peggy Palmer
Phyllis Pasley
Sondra Paulson
Virginia Perrin
Mary Pritchett
Jeanette Quinn
Allison Rasmussen
Karen Renton
Ruth Rice
Pamela Roberts
Jay Rogers
Mark Romig
Deborah Root
Ronald K. Rydell
Arlene Sands
Norm Sands
Ruth Ann Scanzillo
Rhonda Schilling
Rita Schnell
Maria Schwab
Donna Schwinn-Roblee
Audrey Seidman
Joan Sidor
Theo Smith
Allan Stephens
Rob Stow
Joanne Terry
Lydia Toliver
May Tuan Tucker
Barbara-Jo Vanderkraats
Rachel Veenker
Judy Vincent
Jeff Ward
David Watkins
Judy Wellert
Lyle Whybrew
Lessie Williams
John Mark Wilson
Rebecca L. Wszalek